The Lee and Kenny Everett Cookery Book

The
Lee and Kenny Everett
Cookery Book

Duckworth

First published in 1976 by
Gerald Duckworth & Co. Ltd.
The Old Piano Factory
43 Gloucester Crescent, London NW1

ISBN cloth 0 7156 1137 2
ISBN paper 0 7156 1138 0

Tastily Set by
Specialised Offset Services Limited, Liverpool
and printed in Great Britain by
Unwin Brothers Limited, Old Woking

CONTENTS

PASTA

Spaghetti bolognese	42
Lasagne	43

VEGETABLES

Baked potatoes	46
Cheese dreams	46
Roast potatoes	47
Mashed potatoes	47
New potatoes	47
Potato cakes	47

CAKES, PUDDINGS ETC

Coconut cake	49
Garden party cake	49
Almond tarts	50
Christmas or birthday cake	50
Chocolate cake	51
Banana cake	52
Banana cream filling	52
Cheesecake	52
Lemon roll	53
Candied lemon	54
Bread and butter pudding	54
Steamed roly-poly pudding	54
Baked roly-poly pudding	55
Honey banana creams	55
Banana custard	56
Strawberry trifle	56
Muesli	57
Egg in the hole	58
Lemon curd	59
Banana jam	59
Guacamole dip	60
Egg mayonnaise	60
Anchovy butter	61
Blue cheese butter	61
Pickled onions	61

1,743

"My Dear Reader,

First of all welcome to a book which you will in the fullness of time come to treasure as you treasure your own life. For within these pages there is contained the secret of keeping your entire body and mind in cringing bliss for as long as you can afford to buy food. My own Dear Wife has for many years experimented, pruned and stolen these recipes for the good of the Mouth of Man and in doing this has earned my undying adoration for all the years we've been married. So, plunge on dear friends through the following mouth-watering pages, safe in the knowledge that Cuddly Ken has given these pearls of culinary achievement his full and total seal of approval."

Kenny Everett

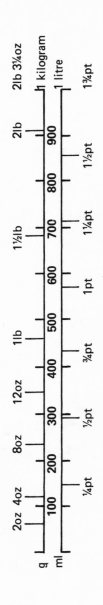

METRIC CONVERSION CHART

SOUPS

QUICK AND EASY POTATO SOUP

"At first glance, this quick and easy soup looks anything but quick and easy. This is because it isn't quick and easy at all. My Wife lied. Opening a tin is both quicker *and* easier, but the difference in taste between this recipe and a tinned soup is the difference between touching the hem of God's frock and having your knees nailed to the floor!"

$\frac{1}{2}$ pint milk
1 small sliced onion
3 medium cooked
    mashed potatoes

$\frac{1}{2}$ pint Oxo stock
seasoning
nut of butter

Simmer onion in milk for about 15 minutes, add beef stock and mashed potatoes, boil all together then season to taste. This is a very quick easy soup and is ideal if you have any leftover mashed potatoes.

LEEK AND POTATO SOUP

"This natty little number is ideal if you've been raving all week and your innards need a rest. Let's face it folks, the stuff one shoves into one's tum these days is quite an onslaught, so to make up for all the curries, chillies and over-spicy stuff that we throw in, give your tubes a treat with this."

1 lb leeks	1 pint Oxo stock
nut of butter	3 small potatoes
1 tbs plain flour	seasoning

Wash leeks well, cut off end and green tops. Slice into fine rings and fry in butter till golden brown. Add raw potatoes sliced very thin. Add stock, simmer for $\frac{3}{4}$ of an hour, stir well with a fork to mash the potatoes and serve.

CREAM OF TOMATO SOUP
(serves 6)

"When you glance at your next can of Tomato Soup, you'll notice a tiny list of things you recognise ... like tomatoes and salt etc., but you'll also see a large list of things that sound like they've just rolled out of a chemical factory. Mother wouldn't have liked it, and Mothers are always right, so try this genius brew containing absolutely no naughty chemicals but instead tons of good honest common or garden vegetables.

P.S. If you're going to eat a lot of these recipes, you'll feel a lot healthier, look a lot rosier, and your stomach'll be so frisky, that when you die, they'll have to beat it to death with a stick!"

Anticipation.

1 stick celery, chopped	2 tbs plain flour
1 carrot (peeled and sliced)	1½ lb tomatoes (peeled and quartered)
1 small onion, chopped	1 pint white stock
2 slices bacon, chopped	bouquet garni
1 oz butter	seasoning
	1 tsp sugar
	2 tbs single cream

Cover tomatoes in boiling water and leave for a minute or two to make peeling easier.

Lightly fry celery, carrot, onion and bacon in butter for about 5 minutes until soft but not browned. Sprinkle flour over and stir well in. Add tomatoes, stock and bouquet garni then cover pan and simmer gently for 30 minutes.

Remove bouquet garni and put whole thing into liquidiser, or push through fine sieve to pulp. Return to pan, season to taste and at last moment of cooking stir in the cream. Make sure the soup doesn't boil after cream is added. Serve at once.

FRENCH ONION SOUP

"First of all let me tell you that contrary to Woman's Hour, *Woman's Own* and every other woman's advisory agency known to man that tells you ways of peeling onions without tears, Lee and I haven't found *one* of them that works yet. And anyway what's wrong with a good cry?

"You may be tempted to eat this dish way before it's completed, as the smell of mere onions frying in butter is enough to send the average human being crawling up the kitchen wall! However battle on till the end and your buds will be well rewarded."

4 large onions
1 tbs plain flour
2½ oz butter
seasoning

2 pints beef stock
  (Oxo)
grated Gruyere cheese
  (or Parmesan)
bread

Peel and slice onions, melt butter in large saucepans and gently fry onions till golden brown. Add flour and continue cooking, stirring all the time till flour is well blended. Cook for about 3 minutes, then gradually stir in stock. Season to taste. Cover pan and cook gently for 20 minutes.

When cooked pour into individual heat-resistant soup bowls. Cut enough rounds of bread for people eating, cut to the size of dishes (just small enough to float on top of the soup). Fry the bread rounds in butter as if making fried bread. Float the fried bread on top of the soup, sprinkle liberally with the cheese then brown under the grill.

SPROUT SOUP
(serves 4)

"If your child refuses to eat Greens there are two remedies. Don't give him any and watch all his teeth drop out, or feed the little dear with this. For a start he'll find it doesn't taste like the nasty old greens from the school dinner centre and B, his hair will grow long and shiny, his teeth will be white and strong and he'll end up in films."

1 lb sprouts
1 pint chicken stock
1 oz butter

½ oz cornflour (if
  necessary)
¼ pint milk
seasoning

Take off outer leaves of sprouts and make cross with knife on stalk. Put sprouts in saucepan with boiling stock. Cook till tender. Put stock and sprouts into liquidiser and pulp; if you have no liquidiser press through a fine sieve. Return pulp to pan, add milk and season to taste. (This soup is lovely with lots of pepper.) If you like your soup thick, it is at this point you add the cornflour, made to a runny paste with a little milk. At the last moment of cooking stir in the butter. Serve at once.

FISH

KIPPERS PLAIN

"Only two ingredients in this one, and one of those is butter and butter is butter is butter ... but kippers are a different kettle of fish. Hunt around for a good wet fish shop and having found one, befriend the owner and have him save all the best kippers for you and get him to give his other customers the grot. This is called being selfish, but it doesn't really matter in this case, as most people after years of fish fingers don't know a good kipper from a bad kipper. You, however, having bought this book, are a connoisseur, and therefore deserve the best. This recipe is just that!"

1 large kipper per person   1 nut butter

Fold kippers into fish shape, wrap in tin foil and bake in oven set at medium heat for 20 minutes. When cooked be careful not to spill natural juice that will gather in foil. Serve with juice poured over and a knob of butter. When cooked this way they do not dry up and shrink, and you don't get the nasty smell that generally accompanies the cooking of kippers.

YORKSHIRE STYLE FISH CAKES

potatoes, large   cod or other white fish

To make one fishcake, slice potato into ¼ inch thick scallops. Take two, sandwich between them a ¼ inch piece of fish (a fraction smaller than the potato slices), coat in flour and dip in batter. Fry in hot fat. When the cakes are half cooked drop a portion of chips in with them, and this slows down the heat and makes sure the fish is cooked through.

This lovely dish was always on sale at our famous Yorkshire chip shops and I missed it very much when I left.

PLAIN MUSSELS

"This recipe contains something that I as a slightly scientifically minded chap don't quite understand. However, Lee is never wrong in my eyes in the kitchen so I guess it's right. It's the bit about the mussels eating the oats overnight. Where would a mussel find oats in the sea??? Ah well, let's skim over that one and simply say that – next to Pirate Radio, it's the best thing that ever came out of water!"

Use 1 lb mussels per person

Scrub mussels under cold tap, scrape off barnacles with small sharp knife and pull out beards. Cover with cold water and leave to stand for one hour or longer. Don't use mussels that are broken or do not close when tapped. I like to use them on day of purchase, but if this is not possible, stand them in a lot of salted water and add a

16

A Dead Taste Bud! Too many fish fingers, instant mashed
potato and tinned soup.

handful of oats (Quaker oats type) – they seem to feed off the oats and grow fatter overnight.

To cook, drain the mussels and put them in a pan on their own – no water; they make their own juice. Put lid on tightly and cook fast for about 7 minutes. When done, they are open and the juice froths up to the top of the pan.

In Yorkshire when I was a child, the steaming hot mussels were placed in a large dish in the centre of the table and we were each given a small bowl containing some of the hot mussel juice; we seasoned it with vinegar and salt and pepper to our own taste and used it as a dip, shelling the mussels ourselves and discarding the shells into an empty bowl placed on the table for this purpose. Our friends find this a fun meal served with hot rolls and butter. We name this the 'Mussel Orgy'. It really is a quick and easy meal to serve.

Variation: Add a crushed clove of garlic and a glass of dry white wine to the pan before cooking. This we call 'Tarted Up Mussel Orgy'! I also serve them cold with drinks, cooking them earlier in the day and discarding the shells then leaving them covered in their own juice with 3 tablespoonsful of vinegar. When ready for serving drain off the juice and stand them in a dish for guests to help themselves. They are much better and cheaper than the pickled ones you buy in jars.

MUSSEL STEW
(serves 4)

"Lee freaks out every time she eats this one. It's the best thing that can ever be done to a mussel apart from allowing it to live. A lot of people make the mistake of adding loads of water to the boiling method. This is wrong and should be shot. The mussels add their own juice and it's a crime to water it down. So there!"

18

3 lb mussels
1 tbs cooking oil
2 large cloves garlic

1 16oz tin tomatoes
1 tbs sugar
2 tbs tomato paste

Clean and cook mussels as for plain mussels, with the addition of $\frac{1}{4}$ inch water in pan before cooking.

Meanwhile, gently cook crushed garlic in oil. Add tomatoes, forced through a sieve to make pulp, or mash all lumps out in the pan. Cook gently for ten minutes.

Meanwhile drain mussel juice into a measuring jug through a sieve to remove any grit. Make juice up to one pint by adding water. Add juice to tomato mix and simmer without lid, until reduced and thickened to a light runny sauce texture. This generally takes thirty minutes. While sauce cooks, remove mussels from shells. Discard shells. When sauce is cooked, divide mussels into soup bowls and pour over the sauce to fill. Serve immediately.

MEAT

POSH TRIPE AND ONIONS
(serves 6)

"I cannot tell a lie. I Hate tripe with a hatred usually saved for mass murderers and Income Tax. I guess it's the look of the stuff, and thinking about where it comes from. However if you like tripe and can keep it down and don't mind the social stigma attached to this disgusting muck, then all I can say is you've got no taste and should be shot!"

2 lb dressed tripe	3 pints chicken stock
3 large onions	$\frac{1}{4}$ pint double cream
1 pint white sauce	bouquet garni
$\frac{1}{2}$ lb button onions	seasoning

Note: I do this version of the meal I was weaned on for when visitors come, but if just for me (Ev doesn't like tripe) I do the traditional version below. Both versions are at their best when served with creamed potatoes and peas.

Button onions are better when fresh, but I have used the frozen packets from shops. Even the ones in white sauce are good. I have often used packet white sauce (2 packets), but of course it's a great satisfaction to have done your own white sauce.

20

Make white sauce, either version. Peel and cook button onions in boiling salted water, unless using frozen ones.

Cut tripe into bite-size pieces, or large if preferred. Cover with stock in a large saucepan with the large onions sliced, add bouquet garni, season lightly, and bring to boil. Cook slowly, for 1½ hours. When cooked take off lid, and if still very sloppy allow stock to reduce. Take out bouquet barni, add white sauce, button onions, check seasoning. Boil 5 minutes and pour into serving dish, add cream and serve at once.

EVERYDAY TRIPE AND ONIONS

"Worse than the above. People who eat this one should be tortured before being shot!"

1½ lb dressed tripe	3 dessertspoons plain
4 large onions	flour
¾ pint milk	seasoning
	¾ pint white stock

Cut tripe in pieces, chop onions and put both in pan. Add milk, stock and seasoning. Bring to boil then simmer on very low heat for 2 hours. Blend flour to a runny paste with a little milk and slowly add to whole dish to thicken.

SUNDAY LAMB DINNER

"This must be eaten on a Sunday at approximately 12.30 while listening to Two Way Family Favourites on the Wireless. The table must have a cloth on it. Tizer may be served, but never anything as strong as booze or

Coca-Cola. Prayers must be short but never avoided, as the least we can do for this recipe is thank God. This is one of the truly great meals of the truly great Nation! (Cue Applause)"

half leg of lamb	potatoes
1 large clove garlic	cabbage or other veg
molasses (or black treacle)	3 tbs Bisto thickening
	$\frac{1}{2}$ basinful of stock
ground rosemary	dripping

Note: I keep all fat previously used for roasting meats in a basin in the fridge and use it every roast as, like soup stock, it gathers flavour and makes the roast potatoes unforgettable.

Put dripping into large roasting tin in middle of pre-heated oven (400 degrees or mark 6).

Peel potatoes and cut into roasting size, put into saucepan with water and boil about 12 minutes (or until cooked through but not fallen).

With point of knife make small inserts in lamb (about 8, evenly spread). Slice garlic clove into slivers and insert a sliver into each slit. Coat the whole joint thinly in molasses then sprinkle with rosemary.

When fat is hot, put lamb into tin with drained potatoes around it, and spoon fat all over. Return tin to oven and cook 30 minutes.

Meanwhile mix Bisto with water in jug till smooth and runny. Set aside. Chop cabbage, or chosen veg. When 30 minutes is up, turn meat and potatoes, baste and return to oven.

Wait 20 minutes, then bring 1 pint of unsalted water to boil and cook cabbage, uncovered, for 10 minutes. When cabbage is done, remove meat and potatoes from tin and put on serving dish in turned off oven to keep warm (do

British Sunday Dinner. A Truly British Bud.

not cover). Drain dripping back into stock fat basin carefully, leaving all meat juices in tin. Drain cabbage into colander held over meat tin, mixing cabbage water with meat juices. Put cabbage into serving dish and put in oven (I mash our cabbage with salt, pepper and butter).

Add Bisto mixture to veg and meat juices in meat tin gradually, stirring constantly to prevent lumps forming. You may not need all the Bisto mixture. I carry on adding it until I reach the thickness we like, which is very thick. Serve.

SUNDAY ROAST BEEF DINNER

Rub garlic salt all over meat and cook as for Lamb Dinner above. Serve with Yorkshire pudding (see recipe below).

YORKSHIRE PUDDING

"Lee's Mother Elsie, God rest her, used to serve these Northern things as a meal in themselves. Nowadays however, they are but a small part of the Show. The thrill of Yorkshire Puds is not so much in the taste of them as in the being able to make them at all. A well-made Yorkshire Pudding is as much a work of art as the Sistine Chapel roof, which rather resembles a giant camp Yorkshire Pud. Treat the humble pud with respect. Venus de Milo would've given her right arm for one and in fact did just that."

5 oz plain flour
pinch of salt
1 tbs dripping

$\frac{1}{2}$ pint milk and water
mixture ($\frac{3}{4}$ water $\frac{1}{4}$ milk)

Note: Many people fail badly with this dish, but in fact it is the most simple thing to make. The secret is to use more water than milk, and to make the batter at least an hour before needed and leave to stand covered. The most important thing is to not put too much batter in. I cover the dish I'm using with about $\frac{1}{4}$ inch batter. Then make sure the oven is 450 degrees (gas mark 8) and put the pudding at the top (or the hottest part of oven). If cooking with Sunday joint always make sure the pudding is higher in the oven than the meat.

Put flour in mixing bowl sieved together with salt, make a well in flour and gradually add milk and water mixture, mixing to a smooth paste. Heat the dripping (make sure it is very hot) and put in the batter in a thin layer. Cook for 30 minutes to coincide with the start of the meal. When cooked the pudding should have risen to a large puff with a hollow centre (none of that sad paste inside that I meet so regularly when eating out).

In Yorkshire we serve this as a starter with the meat course to follow.

A very good variation of this dish is to grate an onion into the batter. This will not rise like ordinary pudding, but makes a nice change. I use the onion version when making Toad in the Hole.

TOAD IN THE HOLE

"Take a rather old toad a bit on the fat side and fry gently on both sides until deep golden green. Garnish with freshly chopped rat and cram into a handy hole. Well, that's one way; another is shown below. A trifle tamer, but probably a lot tastier."

Precook $\frac{1}{2}$ lb sausages in frying pan or under grill, making sure they get rid of most of the fat. Cook till almost ready to eat, according to your own preference. Place sausages in a large baking tin, evenly spaced, add some of the hot fat and pour over the batter mixture. Cook in oven as for Yorkshire pudding. I generally cook the sausages in the tin in the oven, pouring off a bit of the fat when they're done. This makes the whole thing easier.

A nice variation of Toad in the Hole is to substitute lamb chops for the sausages. Cook as for Toad.

LANCASHIRE HOT POT
(serves 4)

"It really does pay to have one of those slicing machines in the house for this recipe as before we got one, Lee used to lose more time and fingers hanging over the slicing board than over the rest of the recipe.

"The recipe was formulated and refined by Northerners during hundreds of years of scraping and poverty and is therefore quite cheap considering the delicious taste. Whilst eating this dish, sing selections of old Beatle melodies for that extra twist of Ethnickness."

1 lb lean stewing lamb	1½ pints white stock
2 lb potatoes	salt and pepper
3 medium onions	

Note: I buy ½ shoulder of lamb, the cheapest, then I use the bone for soup or white stock and render down the fat for stock dripping.

Heat oven to 325 degrees or mark 3. Cut lamb into small pieces, peel potatoes and slice into thin scallop shapes, peel onions and slice them in same manner as the potatoes. Use a large casserole, I use one 9" long by 6"

26

An undernourished taste bud.

across by 3″ deep. Grease the casserole dish to prevent sticking, then put a layer of potatoes to cover bottom of dish, then a layer of meat then a layer of onions; salt and pepper liberally. Carry on in these layers until the dish is almost full, not forgetting the seasoning between each layer. Pour stock over and put lid on casserole and cook in coolest part of oven for $3\frac{1}{2}$ hours, then put a few little dabs of dripping on top and finish cooking without lid for $\frac{1}{2}$ hour.

CHICKEN AND POTATO PIE
(serves 4)

"Think of a Chicken ... Boring. Right? Right! Well, here's a natty way of introducing some taste into this battery bird. For a start try and get a fresh one. This might involve a few months searching up the Amazon, but if you find one it'll be well worth while. Chickens are thick, so don't feel too bad about throwing one into a pie. Potatoes are pretty stupid too!"

1 small chicken (or 4 pieces)	1 oz butter
2 medium carrots	1 pint white stock
2 medium onions	1 glass white wine
$\frac{1}{4}$ lb mushrooms	pinch parsley
2 tbs cooking oil	1 bayleaf
2 peeled tomatoes	seasoning
$1\frac{1}{2}$ oz flour	milk
1 tbs lemon juice	$\frac{1}{2}$ lb shortcrust pastry
	$\frac{1}{2}$ lb potatoes

Skin chicken. Peel and dice carrot, peel and chop onion small. Heat oil in saucepan and lightly brown onion, carrot and chicken. Add wine, stock, bayleaf and parsley, season and simmer for 1 hour.

Meanwhile make pastry, or use the frozen type (I

28

make my own up when I have a spare afternoon; I make 2 lb at one time, then I freeze it in half pound flat pieces). Cook diced potatoes through.

When chicken is cooked, strain juice into a measuring jug. Put all cooked vegetables into deep pie dish (being careful to remove bayleaf). Take chicken off bone and cut into bite size pieces, add to vegetables. Rub frying pan with butter and quickly fry quartered mushrooms, add these to rest of vegetables. Top the lot off with the cooked potatoes, drained.

Melt butter in saucepan, add flour and chicken liquid made up to 1 pint with milk, and whisk over very low heat to prevent lumps forming. Cook, still whisking, till it becomes a light runny white sauce. Add seasoning – not too much salt. Pour sauce over chicken mixture, leave to go cool.

Roll pastry out to about $\frac{1}{4}$ inch thick (we like it $\frac{1}{2}$ inch thick). Put pastry lid on dish, sealing to sides of dish with milk. Bake 35 minutes at 450 degrees (gas mark 8) or until pastry browns. I coat top of pie in milk which browns it quicker.

This dish can also be made in individual pies.

CORNED BEEF HASH
(serves 4)

"This is basically a basic sort of dish, basically, but can be tarted up like mad, should your heart so desire. Throw a leek in or a carrot or any old bits of anything edible in the veg line. Good recipe for misers and cheapskates."

1½ lb potatoes	1 pint Oxo stock
2 large onions	2 tbs milk
1 tin corned beef (12 oz)	nut of butter
	seasoning

29

Peel and quarter potatoes and boil in Oxo stock until cooked through. If 1 pint doesn't cover potatoes top up with water.

Meanwhile peel and chop onions and fry gently till thoroughly cooked but not brown. Drain potatoes and mash with milk and butter till smooth, mix onions in with potatoes, flake corned beef and mash into potato mixture making sure it's evenly distributed.

Form mixture into pancake shape, either one large or 4 small. Fry till crisp on underside. Meanwhile heat grill to full, then brush top with butter, put pan under grill and brown topside. Serve immediately. We eat this with baked beans.

You can cook the mixture up to frying stage earlier in the day then just fry when needed.

MEAT AND TATER PIE
(serves 4)

"This giant meal is a real moneysaver. As made in days of yore by ancient Britons. Unfortunately they didn't have Oxo, that wonderful little cube that really makes this meal supreme. (Dear Oxo, send a free crate of cubes for this free plug.) P.S. Dear Bisto, my wife also uses your stuff, so how about a TV commercial? Tessa Blackburn's gravy looks like the Mersey compared with ours!"

$2\frac{1}{2}$ lb potatoes	1 large onion
seasoned flour	1 pint Oxo stock
$\frac{1}{2}$ lb shortcrust pastry	1 lb steak and kidney
Bisto	

Peel and cut potatoes into small pieces and boil in salted water to cook right through. Drain and set aside to cool.

Cut beef and kidney into bite size pieces and coat

completely in seasoned flour, put into saucepan with chopped onion and stock, bring to boil then simmer for 1 hour.

Lift meat and onion out of stock with a large perforated spoon. Put meat into a deep pie dish, put potatoes on top, add a little juice from stock to moisten.

Roll out pastry to thickness preferred and put on piecrust top, seal edges with milk to sides of dish. Paint pastry with milk then bake in pre-heated oven 450 degrees (gas mark 8) for 40 minutes or until crust is browned. When almost cooked, mix Bisto with a little cold water and thicken the stock that the meat was cooked in over a low light. We like our gravy thick but you can adjust as you like by the amount of Bisto used. Serve with green vegetables.

QUICK AND EASY LIVER PATE

"Some people suffer from the opinion that paté is reserved only for lords and queens and people who say to their butlers "Hudson, throw another peasant on the fire". This is simply a lie and should be shot. Paté for the proletariat I say! Once you've made it, you can keep running to the fridge for a quick nibble, as it's delicious on the end of a piece of cold toast."

1 onion	2 oz butter
1 large clove garlic, crushed	2 rashers bacon
8 oz pig's liver (or calves')	

Fry onion and garlic in half the butter till almost cooked through, not browned. Add bacon and liver to pan and lightly cook till liver is still pink inside. (If you slice liver

into thin pieces you only need cook for about 1 minute.)
Put all into liquidiser, melt remaining butter in pan and
pour in with liver. Liquidise, or press through a sieve.

I serve this paté hot on crisp toast but it is also
delicious cold.

LIVER AND ONION CASSEROLE

"Whatever I say about this recipe, once you've eaten it
you'll say I've understated. So ... "

2 pieces calves' liver per person	1 tbs Bisto
1 pint water	1 tbs cooking oil
2 medium onions	$\frac{1}{4}$ tsp pepper
seasoned flour	1 peeled tomato

Note: I keep a jar of seasoned flour and use it when
coating, it saves a lot of wastage. For this recipe I get my
butcher to cut the liver into $\frac{1}{2}$ inch thick slices.

Fry onions in the oil till transparent; meanwhile coat
liver in seasoned flour. Just before onions are cooked, add
liver to pan and fry quickly on each side, not to cook, just
to seal in the juices. Add tomato chopped. Add water to
the pan, cook for 1 minute. Transfer liver mixture to a
casserole and add the pepper. Cook in oven at 250
degrees or gas mark $\frac{1}{2}$ for 45 minutes. Mix Bisto to a
runny paste in water and add to the casserole, stirring
well. Cook for 15 more minutes. Serve with creamed
potatoes and peas, or veg of your choice.

CREAMED KIDNEYS
(serves 4)

"There are only two good things to do with a kidney — donate it or cream it. This recipe will have you on your back screaming for more. Kidneys are full of vitamins, but vitamins don't taste of anything. This recipe does. It tastes of kidneys. And rice. Well, the rice tastes of rice. However, rice doesn't really taste of anything either, so mix it up with the kidneys. Eat and freak!"

2 oz butter
1 chopped onion
6 skinned lambs'
   kidneys
3 oz sliced mushrooms

4 tbs red wine
2 tbs Worcester sauce
seasoning
$\frac{1}{4}$ pint single cream

Melt butter and cook onions till clear; quarter kidneys and remove fat; add to onions with red wine, sauce, seasoning and mushrooms. Cook for 10 minutes or until kidneys are cooked through. Put a little liquid from pan into the cream, then gently stir cream into kidney mixture. Simmer for 1 minute. Then serve on a bed of rice.

HAMBURGERS
(makes about 10)

"America has given us many good things. Marilyn Monroe, Elvis Presley, Coca-Cola, Woody Allen, Star Trek and Hamburgers. There are a lot of Hamburger joints around London, and the Sunday supplements have thoroughly researched each one. They needn't have bothered, because folks, Tantatatatataaaaaarrrnnn!!! (trumpet effects) here lies the best Hamburger recipe the world has ever known. Tender, Juicy, Big, Wide. You'll thrill to Lady Lee's mouthwatering Epic. You'll bend over backwards with onion and ketchup. You'll tremble with thrillness as your taste buds send messages of congratulations to your brain for having bought this book.''

1 medium onion
1 lb minced beef
1 lb minced pork
seasoned flour
1 tbs cummin powder
   or home-ground
   cummin seeds

1 egg
1 tsp ground allspice
seasoning
oil for frying

Note: I get my butcher to mince the beef and pork together for me. The seasoned flour is for coating. I buy a coarse flour for this. Matzo meal is best, but ordinary flour will do just as well.

Peel onion and chop very small. Mix all other ingredients except flour and oil. Make sure the mixture is evenly mixed. Roll into balls and flatten out into hamburger shapes. Coat in the seasoned flour and fry to taste. Serve with fried onions and baps.

We like ours fairly rare, still pink inside. We also like them very thick (about 1 inch) – this makes a substantial meal.

CHICKEN CURRY
(serves 4)

"Whenever you say to yourself 'Cripes, what shall we eat tonight?' that means it's time for a Curry. India with all its Taj Mahals and white elephants has never come up

34

A taste bud owned by someone who bought this book.

with anything as Orgasmic as this Lady Lee Special. The ingredients are obtained best of all in Southall, Middlesex where there is a large Indian community but any good delicatessen should have all that is required. Don't jump about after eating this."

1 jointed chicken	1 tsp turmeric
2 oz butter	1 tsp cummin powder
2 sliced onions	$\frac{1}{2}$ pint chicken stock
3 shelled cardamoms	1 8oz carton plain
2 tsp ground	yoghourt
coriander	2 tsps coconut
1 tsp chilli powder	salt
squeeze of lemon	1 tsp garam masala
1 tbs curry powder	
1 heaped tsp plain	
flour	

Note: Use desiccated coconut. Infuse in half a teacup of boiling water, then use water as well as coconut.

Remove skin from chicken and discard. Put chicken in pan, pour over stock, add salt and cook gently without lid till chicken is tender. Meanwhile heat butter and fry onions till golden brown. Crush cardamoms under a knife blade and mix together with rest of spices. Add spices and flour to onions in pan and cook gently for about 1 minute.

At this point I take chicken off the bone, but some people prefer it on the bone. Add chicken to mixture when it has cooked enough to reduce and thicken, about 10 minutes before cooking is completed. If you add chicken too soon the meat will shred.

In last 5 minutes of cooking add yoghourt, coconut and lemon. Serve on a bed of rice.

BEEF CURRY

1 lb stewing beef
rest of ingredients as above excluding chicken

Cut beef into cubes and cook in saucepan with onions, in own juice, with lid on tight for 15 minutes. Add spices, then stock, and continue as for chicken curry.

TANDOORI CHICKEN

"This is the one where the chicken is red all over and very spicy and will send your taste buds on a trip into the nether regions. It must be a great source of comfort to a chicken knowing that maybe one day it'll become tandooried. Don't make this meal for just anybody. Make it for someone you want to fall in love with you and they surely will. I hope they serve this in Heaven. If they don't, I ain't goin'!"

2 lb roasting chicken
1 large onion
3 cloves garlic
1 inch fresh ginger (or tinned)
1 tsp coriander powder
1 tsp cummin powder

1½ oz butter
¼ tsp chilli powder
1½ tsp salt
5 oz plain yoghourt
2 tsps vinegar
2 tsps Worcester sauce
juice of 2 lemons
1 tsp garam masala

Make cuts along chicken breast and legs. Finely mince onion, garlic and ginger and mix to a paste; add coriander, cummin, chilli and salt. Beat yoghourt with the vinegar and Worcester sauce; add the juice of 1 of the lemons, mix well with the spices. Rub mixture well into the chicken and into the cuts; put chicken in a bowl and pour over rest of sauce. Put into fridge or in cool place to soak up flavour for at least 6 hours. I do all this 1 day before cooking and leave to stand overnight.

When chicken is thoroughly marinated, melt 1 oz butter in large casserole. Add chicken and sauce and cook in oven, preheated to 425 (gas mark 7), for 1 hour. To serve, brush chicken with remaining butter and sprinkle with garam masala. Serve with potatoes and salad or vegetables. We eat it with baked potatoes with curry butter and a salad on the side. To make curry butter, mix 4 oz soft butter with 3 (or more) tsp curry powder.

Chicken done like this makes a lovely change, and gives flavour to those awful battery chickens, if one has to buy them. Try tandoori chicken cold too – it's delicious either way.

CHILLI CON CARNE
(serves 6)

"Now we come to the top of the tree. The Piece of Resistance, the Best Meal that has ever existed in the Universe since the beginning of time. Many's the time Lee has served this to showbiz agents and TV executive friends of mine and soon after this, contracts and offers of work flow in like confetti. I could live on this stuff forever. Lee's chilli con carne has saved our marriage many a time, as the thought of never having it again has struck horror into the very heart of my taste buds. You MUST try it. It'll make a new man of you. Even if you're a woman."

Chilli con carne.

1 lb best stewing beef	4 chopped garlic cloves
1 lb pork (lean)	1 level tbs plain flour
2 large onions (sliced)	2 tbs paprika (less if not so hot)
1 tbs chilli powder	1 16 oz tin tomatoes
1 pint boiling water	1 bay leaf
1 tbs oregano	1 tsp whole cummin seed
2 heaped tbs cummin powder	salt and pepper
1 tin red kidney beans	
3 Oxo cubes	

Note: I always cook this dish one day before I need it as it is even better re-heated.

Cut beef and pork into cubes, put into large pan with sliced onions and chopped garlic. (I use a garlic crusher, a very good buy from any hardware shop.) Put lid tight on pan and simmer over very low heat for 15 minutes. Meanwhile, put chilli powder, crumbled Oxo cubes, oregano, cummin powder, flour, paprika, bay leaf and cummin seeds onto a dish together and set aside: Open the tin of red kidney beans and drain liquid off, set aside, open tin of tomatoes and boil the water ready for next stage.

When 15 minutes are up you should find the meat has made a good amount of juice. Add the dish of ready measured out herbs and stir into juice. The smell at this stage is a delight. Add red beans and boiling water, and put tomatoes through a sieve over pan, adding to rest of ingredients. Bring mixture to boil then simmer for 1 hour. Season to taste then return to heat and simmer for another hour.

Set aside over night then just warm up 15 minutes before needed, to coincide with boiling of rice. Serve on a bed of rice.

This dish is very, very hot but lovely for a dinner party as you only need put the pan on when your guests decide they are hungry.

PORK SPARERIBS
(serves 4)

"Make a real Pig of yourself! This is not a dainty dish, so if you know any old queens, don't set it before one. There is only one place on Earth that comes anywhere near providing spareribs as delicious as my wife's and that's Trader Vic's restaurant in the London Hilton, and they give you funny looks if you go in just for spareribs. The prices are so high in there, you have to take out a Mortgage for a full meal."

4 lb pork spareribs	2 tbs butter
1 cup molasses	2 tbs malt vinegar
1 medium chopped onion	2 tbs salad oil
juice of 1 orange	2 tbs brown steak sauce
3 tbs minced orange rind	1 tsp prepared mustard
4 clove garlic	1 tsp Worcester sauce
$\frac{1}{2}$ tsp hot pepper sauce	$\frac{1}{2}$ tsp pepper
$\frac{1}{2}$ tsp salt	

Put spareribs on a rack in roasting tin and lightly sprinkle with salt, cover with tinfoil and bake in oven at 325 degrees (gas mark 3) for 1 hour. Meanwhile mix all other ingredients in a pan and bring to the boil, then simmer for 5 minutes. Set aside.

When ribs are cooked, remove from oven and turn oven up to 400 degrees (gas mark 6). Pour off all excess fat and spread ribs with some of the mixture previously prepared. Bake in oven, basting with rest of sauce every 15 minutes, for 45 minutes in all, or until glazed. Serve hot.

This is generally served as a starter, but we have it as a main course with baked potatoes and side salad.

PASTA

SPAGHETTI BOLOGNESE

"Lee and I take the easy way out on this one. When it's served up, we chop the long awkward spaghetti into handy two-inch bits with a fork and spoon. That way, we can stop worrying about the mechanics of getting it on the fork and concentrate on the eating thereof. Needless to say, it's delicious. But not only that, it's a saving in the long run. It's so filling, that you won't want anything to eat after this for at least a day."

1 16 oz tin tomatoes
1 lb lean minced beef
1 large finely chopped
  carrot
8 oz finely chopped
  mushrooms
2 garlic cloves
2 oz butter or
  margarine

½ pint Oxo stock
  (made with 2
  cubes)
2 wineglasses red wine
2 finely chopped
  onions
1 tbs flour (plain)

For the pasta:
long Italian spaghetti (about 2 oz per person)
lots of boiling salted water

Note: I always cook this 1 day before needed, as it gets better each time it's warmed up. I use a vegetable chopper to prepare the veg; you can purchase them from any hardware shop, and they are very cheap and one of the best used things in my kitchen. Don't use wine that you wouldn't like the taste of when drinking it; I find a cheap but pleasant-tasting one and stick to it every time. I buy parmesan cheese by the $\frac{1}{2}$ lb piece from delicatessens, grate fine and store in a jar — it lasts ages and is much cheaper than the small drums or packets you buy ready grated.

Melt butter in a saucepan, taking care not to burn it. Gently fry crushed garlic, mushrooms, flour and carrots for a few minutes. Add the mince, crumbling it into pan so as not to end up with lumps. Add rest of ingredients. Simmer for 2 hours, season to taste. Set aside until needed. This can be eaten the same day, but it really is worthwhile doing as I do.

To make the pasta, bring pan of salted water to the boil. Gradually lower pasta into water, bending as the submerged part softens. Boil till soft but firm (about 12 minutes) — test by squeezing between thumb and finger. Drain into large sieve, and if it has to wait before being served stand the sieve over the pan it was cooked on on a very low heat. Do take care not to overcook, as pasta goes sticky and clots in nasty lumps if you do.

LASAGNE
(serves 12)

"Pronounced lassanya. To be eaten with an Italian accent. You may think that the preparation of this one is a little complex and would be better handled by a team of brain surgeons. Not so, dear reader! It not only serves an awful lot of people *and* is freezable but will win you the undying love of all who sample this wild sexy dish. Even Italians don't make it as good as this."

Start by making the meat sauce.

meat sauce

1 lb minced beef	1 6oz tin tomatoes
1 large chopped onion	2 tbs tomato paste
1 clove garlic	$\frac{1}{4}$ pint water
6 sprigs parsley	2 bay leaves
2 tbs olive oil	

Sauté onion, garlic (crushed), parsley in the oil till transparent. Stir in pulped tomatoes, tomato paste, water and bay leaves. Crumble the minced beef into the mixture. Cover pan and simmer for 1 hour stirring occasionally. When cooked, remove bay leaves and set aside. Whilst this is cooking make the cheese sauce as follows.

cheese sauce

1 small chopped onion	1 pint hot milk
2 oz butter	4 oz grated parmesan
3 tbs plain flour	cheese
2 egg yolks	pinch salt

Sauté onion in the butter until transparent, not brown. Blend in 3 tbs flour and cook roux for about 2 minutes, stirring all the time. Add hot milk, parmesan cheese and salt. Cook over low heat until it thickens. Beat the egg yolks in a bowl and stir a little of the cheese mixture into them, beating briskly. Add eggs to rest of mixture. Set aside. Now cook the pasta.

1 lb lasagne pasta

Put carefully into a pan of boiling salted water, making sure that pasta doesn't stick together. Follow directions on packet.

44

In a large casserole, put a layer of pasta on the bottom. Cover with a layer of meat sauce and cover that with a layer of cheese sauce. Continue in this manner until the dish is full, ending with a layer of cheese sauce. Bake in a preheated oven, 325 degrees (gas mark 3) for 20 minutes, then finish off under a hot grill to brown the top. Serve at once.

Note: I always make this dish in large quantities and freeze some of it in an oven-proof freezer dish.

WHEN IN LONDON, LISTEN TO CAPITAL RADIO 194m 95.8 VHF

CAPITAL RADIO

Keep your ears well fed too!

VEGETABLES

Always buy vegetables as fresh as possible, and don't wash them until ready to use as they keep better dirty.

When cooking them always remember if it grows above the ground (e.g. cabbage) it should be cooked without a lid, if it grows below the ground boil with a lid.

Green veg should be put into already boiling water and root veg into cold water.

BAKED POTATOES

Try to get King Edwards – they bake best. Ask for large ones. Scrub well and cut a fairly deep cross on top. Bake in preheated over at 450 degrees (gas mark 8) for $1\frac{1}{4}$ to $1\frac{1}{2}$ hours.

When cooked squeeze to open cross and serve with large nut of butter on top.

CHEESE DREAMS

Bake potato as above then scoop out centre and mash with seasoning and butter to taste. Top with grated cheese and grill till top is brown.

ROAST POTATOES

Peel and cut potatoes into pieces roughly the same size. Boil in salted water for about 15 minutes or until cooked through. Drain the potatoes and put into hot fat in preheated oven. Cook at 400 degrees (gas mark 6) for about 1½ hours, basting well from time to time, until crisp on outside and soft inside. Never cover whilst cooking or they will go soft and soggy.

MASHED POTATOES

Peel and cut into roughly even pieces, boil about 20 minutes till cooked through. Drain and mash to smooth consistency, add butter and milk to taste and salt and pepper. 1½ lbs makes about 1lb mashed. I usually find 1 lb is enough for 2 people.

NEW POTATOES

Scrub dirt from spuds taking care not to break skins. Boil in salted water for about 20 minutes till soft. Drain and put back into saucepan with a generous nut of butter. Cook gently for 5 minutes, shaking from time to time to coat evenly. Add chopped mint and serve in skins.

POTATO CAKES

½ lb potatoes	salt
1 medium onion	¼ lb plain flour
1 egg	dripping for frying

Coarsely grate raw potato and onion, add salt and flour, mix well then add beaten egg to make a kind of batter.

Heat dripping in frying pan, add mixture, spreading out into pancakes. Fry till brown on both sides.

CAKES, PUDDINGS, ETC.

COCONUT CAKE

6 oz butter	3 eggs
6 oz sugar	7 oz plain flour
3 tbs milk	1 tsp baking powder
pinch salt	vanilla essence
3 oz desiccated	
coconut	

Cream together butter and sugar till light in colour, add eggs one at a time mixing all the time. Sieve together flour and baking powder and mix with other, add milk, salt, essence and coconut. Pour into cake tin. Bake in preheated oven, 375 degrees (gas mark 4-5) for $1\frac{1}{2}$ hours.

GARDEN PARTY CAKE

3 oz butter	1 packet raspberry or
1 egg	strawberry
3 tbs sugar	blancmange
4 tbs plain flour	1 tsp baking powder

Cream butter in a warm mixing bowl, add egg and beat together. Add sugar, flour, blancmange and baking powder, mixing well together. Pour mixture into baking tin and bake at 375 degrees (gas mark 4-5) for $1\frac{1}{4}$ hours.

Turn out onto wire rack to cool.

When cool cut in half across centre and spread with cream or jam. Put cake back together, melt a small bar of chocolate in a basin over hot water and coat top of cake.

ALMOND TARTS

8 oz shortcrust pasty	1 tbs water
jam	2 oz ground almonds
2 large egg-whites	4 oz castor sugar
few drops almond	
essence	

Roll out pastry thinly, cut in rounds with a pastry cutter and line greased tart tins. Put a tiny knob of jam in each, about half a teaspoonful.

In a mixing bowl whisk the egg whites till stiff and peaks form, gently add water and carefully stir in the ground almonds, castor sugar and almond essence. Fill pastry cases with mixture. Roll any leftover pastry into thin strips between thumb and finger and lay in cross pattern over each tart, making sure you secure pastry to pastry.

Bake in a preheated oven, 400 degrees (gas mark 6) at the top of the oven for 25 to 30 minutes or until browned.

CHRISTMAS OR BIRTHDAY CAKE

$\frac{3}{4}$ lb brown sugar	2 oz candied peel
$\frac{3}{4}$ lb butter	4 oz glazed cherries
6 eggs	$\frac{1}{4}$ lb chopped almonds
1 lb plain flour	$\frac{3}{4}$ tsp allspice
1 lb sultanas	2 tbs dark treacle
1 lb currants	1 glass brandy (or
6 oz raisins (stoned)	more to taste)

Note: I like to bake this cake at least a month before needed as it gets better with age. I also make it very moist before storing, in the following way: pierce with a fine skewer all over and slowly pour over 1 glass of brandy, so as to soak into the holes. Wrap the cake in tinfoil and store in a cake tin.

Cream together butter and sugar till light in colour. Add treacle, then the eggs one at a time, beating to a smooth paste. Put in rest of ingredients and mix evenly. Line the inside of a large cake tin with greaseproof paper and pour in cake mixture. Bake in a preheated oven at 300 degrees (gas mark 2) for 4 hours, just below middle of oven. When cooked turn onto a wire rack to cool.

CHOCOLATE CAKE

4 oz soft margarine	1 tbs golden syrup
4 oz sugar	vanilla essence
5 oz self-raising flour	1 $\frac{1}{2}$ oz chocolate
2 beaten eggs	powder
	milk to soften

Cream together margarine, sugar, golden syrup and vanilla till soft and light in colour. Sieve together flour and chocolate powder and mix with other mixture. Add beaten eggs and enough milk to soften. Turn into cake tin and bake in preheated oven at 375 degrees (gas mark 4-5) for 20 minutes. Turn out onto wire rack to cool. When quite cool, melt a small bar of chocolate over a double boiler pan and spread over the top of the cake.

For a change you can also cut the cake in half horizontally and spread with thick whipped cream flavoured with powdered chocolate to taste.

BANANA CAKE

2 eggs	1 tsp vanilla essence
2 bananas	½ tsp salt
10 oz sugar	8 oz self raising flour
4 oz butter	½ tsp baking powder

Put eggs, bananas, sugar, butter, vanilla and salt into a large mixing bowl and beat together to form a creamy even mixture. Sift flour with baking powder and combine well with banana mixture. Pour into large baking tin and bake at 375 degrees (gas mark 4) for about 45 minutes. Cook on wire rack.

BANANA CREAM FILLING

1 ripe banana	1 tsp nutmeg
2 oz castor sugar	¼ pint double whipping cream

Whip cream till thick, mash banana till smooth, mix with cream, sugar and nutmeg. Cut cake in half and pour cream onto bottom half; replace top.

CHEESECAKE

8 oz plain flour	8 oz cream cheese
6 oz butter	grated peel of 1 lemon
3 egg yolks	juice of half a lemon
2 oz castor sugar	2 oz currants
3 stiffly beaten egg whites	

Make a dough of flour, butter, 1 egg yolk. Roll out like pastry and line a cheesecake tin. Cream 8 oz cream cheese with remaining 2 egg yolks, add grated rind and lemon juice, castor sugar, currants. Carefully fold in the stiff egg whites.

Pour mixture into pastry case and bake in preheated oven at 425 degrees (gas mark 7) for 15 minutes, then turn oven down to 350 degrees (gas mark 4) for a further 40 minutes. Leave to cool before eating.

We love this cake topped with fresh strawberries with jelly poured over and left in the fridge to set.

LEMON ROLL

4 eggs	lemon curd for coating
$\frac{3}{4}$ tsp baking powder	6 oz sugar
$\frac{1}{4}$ tsp salt	12 oz plain flour
castor sugar for coating	1 tsp lemon juice

Beat together eggs, baking powder and salt till thick and pale in colour. Gradually add sugar, beat together till dough rises in bowl (be patient, it's worth it). Fold in flour and add lemon juice. Grease roll tin, line with greaseproof paper. Spread batter evenly in tin and bake in preheated oven at 375 degrees (gas mark 4-5) for 20 to 25 minutes.

Lay out a sheet of greaseproof paper liberally sprinkled with castor sugar. Turn roll out upside down onto castor sugar and peel off first paper. Roll up gently in second paper and put on one side till cold – not in fridge. Then gently unroll, spread with lemon curd (see p.00), and roll up again without the paper. Sprinkle with castor sugar and eat.

I decorate the top (only when entertaining) with candied lemon, recipe below.

CANDIED LEMON

In small pan mix together $\frac{1}{4}$ lb sugar, $\frac{1}{4}$ pint water. Simmer syrup until it begins to thicken. Put 6 slices lemon in the syrup and simmer over very low heat till they are glistening. Turn out onto wax paper till cool, then decorate lemon roll.

BREAD AND BUTTER PUDDING

butter to coat
6 thin slices white
  bread
beaten egg

currants
sultanas
sugar
$\frac{3}{4}$ pint milk

Butter the slices of bread and cut into 3 or 4 pieces. Put a layer of them in a well buttered pie dish, sprinkle on a layer of currants and sultanas mixed and a sprinkling of sugar; carry on in these layers until dish is filled, ending with a layer of bread.

Beat up egg and add to milk, pour over the bread pudding. Let it stand for half an hour to get thoroughly soaked in the milk and egg. Bake in preheated oven at 375 degrees (gas mark 4-5) for 45 minutes. It should by this time have a crisp brown top.

We eat this hot, with fresh cream poured over, but as a child I preferred it with custard poured over.

STEAMED ROLY-POLY PUDDING
(serves 5/6)

8 oz suet pastry   jam or golden syrup

Use Atora shredded suet and follow the direction on the packet for pastry. Roll out the pastry onto a floured board. Remember suet pastry is very sticky so handle as little as possible. Roll into oblong shape about $\frac{1}{4}$ inch thick. Spread the paste with jam or golden syrup, leaving an edge of 1 inch all the way round. Wet the pastry edge with cold water and fingers. Roll the whole thing up and seal all edges firmly. Tie the pudding up in a muslin cloth, allowing enough room for the swelling which takes place in cooking. Steam in double boiler for $1\frac{1}{2}$ hours. Serve with hot custard poured over.

BAKED ROLY-POLY PUDDING

8 oz shortcrust pastry   jam or golden syrup or
                               mincemeat etc.

Make as for steamed pudding except using shortcrust pastry. Put onto greased baking tin and bake in preheated oven at 375 degrees (gas mark 4-5) for 1 hour.
   Serve as above.

HONEY BANANA CREAMS

3 large bananas $\frac{1}{2}$ pint milk
1 large lemon $\frac{1}{4}$ pint water
$\frac{1}{2}$ oz gelatine powder $\frac{1}{2}$ pint double cream
3 tbs honey

Mash bananas together with juice of lemon. Heat honey together with $\frac{1}{2}$ pint milk, stir this into banana mixture. Simmer lemon rind in water for 6 minutes (don't boil it away), then blend this liquid with the gelatine. When clear, add to banana mixture. Put into fridge to cool and thicken.

Fold in 3 tbs of partly whipped cream, spoon into individual dishes and top with rest of cream. Put into fridge till needed.

BANANA CUSTARD

3 bananas   1 pint custard

Make custard as directions on packet. When ready pour into a serving dish and slice the bananas into the custard. Mix well. We like this quick and easy pudding hot, but it's just as nice cold.

STRAWBERRY TRIFLE

14 oz tin of
  strawberries
1 pint custard
1 strawberry jelly

2 tbs sherry (optional)
stale fruit cake or 3
  trifle sponges
$\frac{1}{2}$ pint double
  whipping cream

Note: I always put aside any leftover fruit cake or any that has gone dry and keep it specially for this dish.

Crumble cake or sponges into a large deep serving dish. Drain strawberry juice from fruit into a jug and set aside. Mix sherry and fruit with the cake, making sure the fruit is evenly distributed. Sprinkle 2 tablespoons of the fruit juice over cake to moisten if needed – be careful not to make it too wet.

Make up the jelly with half the amount of hot water given on the packet, stir until all jelly cubes are melted then make up to required measurements by adding the strained fruit juice, and some cold water if necessary. Pour jelly over cake and put in fridge to set.

When jelly is almost set make up custard to directions on packet. Be generous with the custard powder as you need this fairly thick. Put in fridge to cool. When almost cold but still runny, beat custard till smooth and pour over set jelly. Put in fridge to set.

Whip cream till thick and spread evenly over trifle. At this stage I generally hand the whole thing over to my husband who enjoys decorating cakes and trifles. But if you aren't as lucky as me decorate top yourself with fresh fruit, preferably strawberries if in season.

MUESLI
(serves 4)

1 orange	1 banana
juice of 1 lemon	1 oz raisins
2 eating apples	2 oz chopped nuts
3 oz rolled oats	2 tbs clear honey
$\frac{1}{4}$ pint milk	

Remove peel and pith from orange, then chop. Put into bowl with lemon juice. Peel and core apples, grate into the bowl. Peel banana, chop and add to bowl with raisins, nuts, oats, honey and milk. Serve immediately. This makes a lovely summer breakfast. I buy the huge raisins the health food shops keep.

EGG IN THE HOLE

1 slice bread
1 egg
bacon fat

Take
one slice bread
and cut a hole in
centre about 2½"
square. Heat fat (enough
for normal frying pan) and
put in bread and piece from
centre, drop egg (minus shell of
course) into hole in bread. Fry
until white of egg is set
enough to turn, turn whole
thing and fry until egg is
consistency you prefer.
Serve with bacon.
Eggcellent!

LEMON CURD
(enough for one large preserving jar)

8 oz castor sugar
2 eggs
4 oz butter

grated rind of 3
lemons
juice of 2 large lemons

Grate rind from lemons (no pith or white). Squeeze juice from 2 lemons. Put all ingredients into a double saucepan or a basin over hot water. Cook, stirring from time to time until butter and sugar have melted.

Beat eggs well and add them to the mixture. Continue cooking until the mixture coats the back of a wooden spoon. Pour into heated preserving jar, leave to cool then put on lid and store.

BANANA JAM

6 lb bananas
2 lb pears (buy juicy
ones)

2 lemons
4 $\frac{1}{2}$ lb sugar

Peel and cut up bananas. Peel, core pears and cut up to same size as banana pieces. Into your heaviest saucepan (a preserving pan is best but not essential) put 1 lb of the sugar, the juice of the 2 lemons, and the pears, and bring to the boil. Gradually add rest of sugar and the bananas. Stir carefully till jam boils; let it boil fast for 1 hour, keeping it well skimmed of scum.

When cooked mash to a pulp. Heat the jam jars you need and pour in the jam. Leave to cool then put on lids and store.

Our visitors love this jam so much when I serve it atop hot crumpets that I have taken to giving everyone a pot at Christmas.

GUACAMOLE DIP

2 ripe avocados
(chopped)
2 skinned tomatoes
(chopped)
1 bunch spring onions
(sliced)

7 oz can green chilli
peppers (or failing
this 1 tbs chilli
powder)
1 tbs lemon juice
$\frac{1}{4}$ lb bacon

IF YOU DO NOTHING ELSE IN THIS BOOK, DO THIS!
Cook bacon till crumbly crisp. Peel and pit avocado and dice. In a mixing bowl combine avocado and tomatoes, chopped onions, sliced chillies (or powder) and lemon juice. Mash together until as creamy as possible, add crumbled bacon and serve in a large bowl with savoury biscuits to use as a dip. A lovely dish to serve with drinks but do remember it is very hot.

EGG MAYONNAISE

4 eggs
seasoning

6 tbs of your favourite
Mayonnaise
(we like Hellman's)

Place eggs in boiling water and cook for 5 minutes. Place eggs in pan of cold water before shelling to make them easier to handle. Shell eggs, mash with mayonnaise and season to taste.

Yet another lovely dip, this can be served hot or cold. We prefer it with thin crisp cold toast. It is very filling and has saved the day many a time when unexpected faminished guests have arrived. It also makes a lovely tea served hot. Kenny often takes it to work in sandwich form.

ANCHOVY BUTTER

Mix 4 oz soft butter with 6 mashed anchovy fillets and put in fridge.

BLUE CHEESE BUTTER

As above, using 2 oz blue cheese instead of the anchovies. Both are delicious on toast.

PICKLED ONIONS

We love pickled onions but find the shop variety are generally soft, or go that way once opened. The ones you pickle yourself stay crisp and are very cheap and easy to do. Once you've made your own you'll never buy shop ones again.

Buy as many small pickling onions as you think you can manage. I save all my old jam jars etc. especially for this purpose.

Peel onions and stand overnight in brine – 2 rounded tbs salt to each pint of cold water. Make enough to cover the amount of onions you have bought.

Make as much spiced vinegar as you will need; a good way to judge is by the amount of salt water you needed to stand the onions in. Use 1 tbs pickling spices to 1 pint vinegar. Boil the spices in the vinegar for 15 minutes. This sterilises the vinegar and gives it flavour. Leave to go completely cold, and then strain through muslin to rid it of all spice pieces.

Drain your onions and rinse under cold tap. Fill the jars almost to the top and pour in the vinegar. Make little round greaseproof tops $\frac{1}{2}$ inch larger than jar tops, and secure over tops of jars with rubber bands. You can buy tops specially made for this purpose in most hardware shops.